PREFACE

This annotated bibliography reviews the findings of major studies, surveys, and reports that evaluate research done in the past 10 years on Internet crimes against children. This research is categorized into several subtopics: unwanted solicitation for sexual contact or pictures; pornography (children as the subject); harassment and bullying; and unwanted exposure to sexually explicit material. Within each topic, sources are listed chronologically, beginning with the most recent.

Many of the studies extrapolate data from the First (2000) and Second (2005) Youth Internet Safety Survey, which canvassed a nationally representative sample of 1,500 youth ages 10 to 17 to determine the incidence and risk factors of youth exposure to sexual material on the Internet. Researchers also extrapolated data from the National Juvenile Online Victimization Study, which was intended to estimate the incidence of Internet sex crimes against minors during the period 2000 to 2001 that were known to law enforcement officials. The U.S. Department of Justice Office of Juvenile Justice and Delinquency Prevention is currently funding updates to both of these surveys. Other surveys, focus-group studies, literature reviews, and reports commissioned by the U.S. Congress discussed in this bibliography identify the patterns and frequency of criminal use of the Internet involving children and examine the role of law enforcement, parents, and educators in preventing these crimes. The research described in this bibliography also makes recommendations for future studies and legislative remedies.

TABLE OF CONTENTS

PREFACE i

EXECUTIVE SUMMARY 1
    Scope of the Problem 2
    Incidence of Internet Activity 3
    Role of the Family and Other Caregivers 5
    Demographics and Social Characteristics 6
    Law Enforcement 7
    Impact of Internet Crimes 8
    Need for Further Research and Changes in Approach to the Problem 9
    Sources for Annotated Bibliography Executive Summary 10

ANNOTATED BIBLIOGRAPHY 13
    Child Pornography/Exposure to Sexually Explicit Material 13
    Unwanted Sexual Solicitation 23
    Harassment 27
    Cyberbullying 31

EXECUTIVE SUMMARY

Research conducted relative to Internet crimes against children can be grouped into several subtopics: unwanted solicitation for sexual contact or pictures; pornography (children as the subject); harassment and bullying; and unwanted exposure to sexually explicit material. Many of the studies described in this document have been conducted by researchers affiliated with the Crimes Against Children Research Center at the University of New Hampshire who extrapolated data from the First (2000) and Second (2005) Youth Internet Safety Survey. These surveys canvassed a nationally representative sample of 1,500 youth ages 10 to 17 to determine the incidence and risk factors of youth exposure to sexual material on the Internet. Researchers also extrapolated data from the National Juvenile Online Victimization Study, which was intended to estimate the incidence of Internet sex crimes against minors occurring during a one-year period (2000–2001) that were known to law enforcement officials. This bibliography reviews the findings of the studies conducted using these surveys, as well as other surveys conducted for the purpose of identifying the patterns and frequency of criminal use of the Internet involving children. The bibliography also reviews the results of focus-group studies, literature reviews, and reports commissioned by the U.S. Congress.

The purpose of the studies, surveys, and reports reviewed herein was multifaceted. Researchers primarily sought to determine how frequently children view sexually explicit material online and are approached for sexual activity online, as well as the demographics of the vulnerable populations. They also wanted to identify what specific crimes were being committed, and by whom, the role law enforcement plays in curtailing and preventing these activities, and what influence pornography and sexualized material have on the moral values and sexual attitudes of children and youth. They looked at broader issues as well: how children use the Internet generally (as compared with adults) and what role family dynamics and the parent–child relationship play in the prevention of Internet crime. Some of the studies examine a particular aspect of Internet crimes against children. For example, Patricia M. Greenfield, in testimony before Congress, addressed the role of peer-to-peer file-sharing networks. She concludes that the networks are part of a pervasive, sexualized media environment that leads to inadvertent exposure of children and youth to pornography and other adult sexual content. In 2003 the U.S. General Accounting Office reported that child pornography is easily found and downloaded from peer-to-peer networks, confirming observations of the National Center for Missing and Exploited Children.

Other researchers looked at one aspect of online sexual exploitation —the grooming of children by adult predators. Ilene R. Berson and Duncan Brown, in their articles, describe how online predators use deceptive techniques to gain a young child's trust and manipulate him or her into viewing pornography and agreeing to a personal meeting. Janis Wolak, David Finkelhor, and Kimberly J. Mitchell, in "Internet-Initiated Sex Crimes Against Minors," describe characteristics of interactions between Internet predators and their juvenile victims. A year-long survey conducted in 2001 of 129 Internet-initiated sex crimes involving victims age 17 or younger found that face-to-face meetings had occurred in 74 percent of the cases, and 93 percent of those encounters had included sexual contact. Seventy-five percent of the victims were girls. The same authors, writing in "Trends in Youth Reports of Sexual Solicitations, Harassment and Unwanted Exposure to Pornography on the Internet," report survey results indicating that predators use less deception to befriend their online victims than experts had thought. A large majority of the victims who responded to the survey had willingly met and had sexual encounters with the predators.

Scope of the Problem

Communication technologies, such as computers and cell phones, and social-networking sites like My Space enable the rapid creation and dissemination of harassing and pornographic text, pictures, and video. Paris S. and Robert D. Strom note that whereas adults generally use technology only as a tool, adolescents consider technology, including text messaging and chat rooms, to be an essential part of their social life. The results of a 2007 online survey of more than 40,000 students ranging from kindergarten through twelfth grade (Samuel C. McQuade and Neel Sampat) indicate that children begin using the Internet at kindergarten age or younger and that online activities of children in the grades covered by this study include inappropriate behavior and exposure to inappropriate content. Wolak, Mitchell, and Finkelhor note that Internet use by youth age 12 to 17 increased from 73 percent in 2000 to 87 percent in 2005. Cyberbullying (bullying by means of electronic communication, such as instant messaging, e-mail, chat rooms, and cell phones) and victimization begin as early as second grade for some children, and by middle school, students as a group experience or engage in all known forms of cyber abuse and online aggression. Online exchange of sexually explicit content typically begins in middle school.

Researchers (Wilson Huang, Matthew Earl Leopard, and Andrea Brockman) have concluded that the rapid growth of online sexual exploitation of children can be linked to increased Internet accessibility and anonymity, commercialization of exploitative media, and digitization in the production and dissemination of images. These researchers found that, despite legislative initiatives intended to keep pace with the incidence of this type of crime against children, the nature and distribution of child pornography, as well as the characteristics of offenders and victims alike, have remained similar over time and across a wide sample of studies. A 2007 staff report of the U.S. House Energy and Commerce Committee placed the issue of Internet crimes against children in perspective. The committee found that the number of sexually explicit images of children on the Internet was increasing, and that victims were typically younger and the images more violent than in previous years. At the time the report was written, it was estimated that Web sites hosted in the United States accounted for more than half of the child pornography on the Internet, and that commercially available child pornography on the Internet comprised a multibillion-dollar per year industry.

Incidence of Internet Activity

Researchers studied the frequency of exposure to sexually explicit material by boys and girls, how often the youths posted this material, and the frequency of online bullying and harassment activity. Kenzie A. Cameron and Laura F. Salazar found in their study of adolescents ages 14 to 17 that among the participants who reported incidences of exposure to sexually explicit Web sites, most occurred accidentally or unintentionally, via unsolicited e-mails (10 to 20 per day) containing explicit content or links to explicit material. Chiara Sabina, Wolak, and Finkelhor, using data compiled from an online survey of more than 500 college students, found that 72.8 percent (93.2 percent of the male students and 62.1 percent of the female students) of the sample group reported that they had viewed online pornography before the age of 18. Males were found to be more likely to view pornography frequently and to view a variety of images, while females were more likely to be involuntarily exposed to pornography. Wolak, Mitchell, and Finkelhor, in "Unwanted and Wanted Exposure to Online Pornography in a National Sample of Youth Internet Users" reported findings of data taken from the Second (2005) Youth Internet Safety Survey regarding exposure to online pornography. They found that 42 percent of a sample of 10- to 17-year-old Internet users had viewed online pornography during the previous year. Of that 42 percent, 66 percent reported that they had not sought or desired the exposure to pornography.

A survey of more than 1,000 teens and young adults conducted in 2008 and reported by the National Campaign to Prevent Teen and Unplanned Pregnancy revealed that 20 percent of the teens had sent or posted nude or seminude pictures or video of themselves, and 11 percent of young adolescent girls (ages 13 to 16) had done so. Thirty-nine percent of teens reported sending sexually suggestive text messages ("sexting"), and 48 percent of teens reported having received such messages. Mitchell, Finkelhor, and Wolak, in "Online Requests for Sexual Pictures from Youth," used data from the 2005 youth survey to assess the incidence of soliciting youth to produce sexually explicit images and post or transmit them online. The authors found that 13 percent of the youth in the study population had received unwanted sexual solicitations over the Internet, and although 4 percent of the youth had received an online request to send a sexual picture of themselves, only one complied. Thirteen percent of the overall survey group received unwanted sexual solicitations that included requests for pictures.

Social-networking Web sites, such as Facebook, My Space, and You Tube, are often used by young persons to harass their peers. Michele L. Ybarra and Mitchell, in "Prevalence and Frequency of Internet Harassment Instigation," extrapolated data from the 2005 youth survey to identify the frequency with which youth ages 10 to 17 engaged in online harassment activity. They found that almost 30 percent of youth had harassed others online during the previous year: 6 percent had frequently harassed others via the Internet; 6 percent had occasionally harassed others online; and 17 percent had harassed others a limited number of times. Amanda Lenhart reports the results of a Parents and Teens 2006 Survey tabulating the incidence of cyberbullying. Researchers found that 32 percent of more than 900 youth (ages 12 to 17) Internet users surveyed had been harassed online. Of this group, 38 percent of the girls and 41 percent of the girls ages 15 to 17 had experienced online harassment, as compared with 26 percent of the boys. Thirty-nine percent of teenagers who provided personal information on a social networking site were the target of harassment. Robin M. Kowalski and Susan P. Limber studied the prevalence of electronic bullying (defined as bullying that takes place through Internet chat rooms, e-mail, instant messaging, or Web sites) among middle school students. Their research found that 11 percent of the students reported being electronically bullied one or more times in the previous two months; 7 percent stated that they had bullied others electronically and had been the victims of electronic bullying; and 4 percent reported that they had bullied others electronically but had not been victims. Chris Moessner reported the results of a national survey of more than 800 children ages 13 to 17 measuring adolescent reaction to cyberbullying, which is defined as the use of the Internet, cell phones, or other technology to send or post text or images intended to hurt or embarrass another person. More than 43 percent of the teenagers in the survey reported that they had experienced cyberbullying in the previous year, with the most common occurrence among those 15 and 16 years old.

Role of the Family and Other Caregivers

Researchers looked at the role parents and other caregivers can play in preventing children from becoming victims of Internet crime, emphasizing that better education programs are needed and that strong communication between adults and children is critical. The study by Chang-Hoan Cho and Hongsik John Cheon found that parents generally underestimate their children's exposure to negative material on the Internet, when in fact children encounter negative content frequently. McQuade and Sampat found that 66 percent of high school students reported that their parents provided no supervision of Internet activities. Cho and Cheon confirm the findings of earlier studies that parents of families exhibiting high levels of cohesion perceive greater control and understanding of their children's Internet use. Similarly, Greenfield found that a warm, communicative parent–child relationship, appropriate sex education, and parental participation in children's Internet activities are critical factors in protecting children from adverse effects of exposure to explicit sexual material. Moessner, in his study of a national survey of cyberbullying by those 13 to 17 years old, suggests that parents can help their children avoid cyberbullies by setting expectations for online behavior and monitoring children's Internet activities. Stefan C. Dombrowski, Karen L. Gischlar, and Theo Durst note that caregivers can access various software tools such as firewall security barriers to monitor a child's online activity and help protect him or her from accessing unsafe Web sites. In addition, they recommend that parents discuss Internet dangers, monitor Internet usage, supervise Internet friendships, and establish an Internet-use contract with their child. Whitney Roban, reporting a 2001 study of more than 1,000 girls ages 13 to 18, concluded that not all girls are receiving pertinent Internet-safety information from their parents, and that half the girls in the study reported breaking Internet rules set by their parents. The study concludes that parents should try to be more proactive in their relationship with their daughters; if they develop a greater understanding of their daughters' online lives, they can better help them navigate negative Internet experiences. The Internet Safety Technical Task Force, in its final report, concludes that in order to address the problem of online safety for minors, adults must use the numerous technologies intended to enhance Internet safety, together with parental oversight, education, social services, and law enforcement.

Demographics and Social Characteristics

Some researchers categorized the incidence of sexual solicitation, unwanted exposure to pornography, and bullying/harassment according to demographic and gender indicators. According to Mitchell, Finkelhor and Wolak, in their evaluation of the second youth survey ("Online Requests for Sexual Pictures from Youth"), youth who are female, black, have close online relationships, or engage in online sexual behavior are more likely than others to receive solicitations for sexual pictures. In another study ("Trends in Youth Reports"), these same authors, extrapolating survey data, found that black youth and low-income families had experienced an increased incidence of sexual solicitation. Unwanted exposure to pornography had increased among those 10 to 12 years old and 16 to 17 years old, boys, and white, non-Hispanic youth. These authors found in another study ("Victimization of Youths on the Internet") that predators had targeted girls for sexual solicitation at almost twice the rate of boys, and youth who were at least 15 years old accounted for nearly two-thirds of incidents of unwanted exposure. They also found that young people at risk for unwanted sexual solicitation, harassment, and exposure to sexual content on the Internet tend to be troubled, older adolescents who use the Internet frequently and engage in high-risk online behavior, although those youth not falling into these categories are at risk as well.

Ybarra and Mitchell studied the social characteristics of offline and online aggressors. Analyzing the results of the first youth survey (2000), they found that although boys commit most incidents of offline harassment, the number of boys and girls who use the Internet to harass their peers is almost equal. Both offline bullies and youth who harass others online often have multiple psychosocial issues: 51 percent of all bullies had been victims of traditional bullying, 44 percent had a poor relationship with their caregiver, 37 percent showed a pattern of delinquency, and 32 percent were frequent substance abusers. These same authors, in "Exposure to Internet Pornography among Children and Adolescents," found that the majority of youth who reported seeking pornography online and offline were male; only 5 percent of females reported having looked for pornography. The majority (87 percent) of those who reported having sought sexual images were older than 14.

Law Enforcement

Researchers studied the role that law enforcement can play in prosecuting online predators and evaluated the effectiveness of their investigations. Brown, in his guide for prosecutors seeking to prosecute online predators, recommends that law enforcement officers acquire probative evidence against the perpetrator, collecting and preserving all evidence of grooming (preparing children for sexual exploitation), such as pornography, Web cameras, and other electronic equipment, in order that prosecutors can present the evidence at trial to show the perpetrator's motivation. Mitchell, Wolak, and Finkelhor, in "Police Posing as Juveniles Online to Catch Sex Offenders," used data from the National Juvenile Online Victimization (NJOV) Study to evaluate the effectiveness of proactive online investigations, in which police investigators use the Internet—posing as minors and often assuming a different gender—to communicate via chat rooms, e-mail, and instant messaging, to interdict youth enticement and child pornography. These investigations were used in 25 percent of all arrests for Internet crimes against children, and resulted in offenders entering pleas in 91 percent of cases. Melissa Wells, along with Finkelhor, Wolak, and Mitchell, used the results of the NJOV Study to highlight two problems faced by law enforcement agencies in making arrests for child pornography: the nature of the child pornography portrayed in the confiscated images may not fit the definitions of existing statutes, and investigators may not be able to determine the age of the children in the images with certainty.

Other problems in law enforcement are discussed in the U.S. House Energy and Commerce Committee staff report. Researchers found that although law enforcement agencies at the state level prosecute 70 percent of all cases involving sexual exploitation of children over the Internet, there is a wide discrepancy among state criminal codes in their treatment of these offenses and in their sentencing practices. Encryption methods, such as anonymizers, significantly interfere with law enforcement's ability to investigate and bring charges against offenders.

Impact of Internet Crimes

Most of the research on Internet crimes against children has focused on quantifying the prevalence of illegal activities and identifying ways of preventing future activities. However, a few researchers have attempted to assess the psychological impact these activities have on young persons, as well the implications for other criminal activity. For example, Cameron and Salazar, in their study of adolescents ages 14 to 17 who regularly use the Internet, determined that both boys and girls reported their perception that exposure to sexually explicit material had no effect on their personal views of either gender or of relationships. Similarly, Sabina, Wolak, and Finkelhor found in their study of college students that only a minority reported that viewing online pornography before the age of 18 had strongly affected their attitudes or emotions about sexuality. On the other hand, Greenfield, who studied the unintended exposure of young people to pornography through peer-to-peer file-sharing networks, concludes that evidence supports the thesis that pornography and sexualized material can influence the moral values, sexual activity, and sexual attitudes of children and youth, including their attitudes toward sexual violence. Neil Malamuth and Mark Huppin studied the relationship between pornography and child molestation. They found that although child molesters (individuals who commit sexual acts against children) use pornography to groom potential victims, pedophiles (individuals who are sexually aroused by children) are less likely to molest a child after viewing pornography. The researchers conclude that whether exposure to a real or virtual child affects a person's behavior depends on a number of risk factors, and that, therefore, no strong cause and effect exists between viewing child pornography and committing sexual molestation of a child.

Michael Bourke and Andres Hernandez, in a very recent study on the relationship between the viewing and collection of child pornography and the commission of a sexual contact crime against a child, reach a different conclusion. The results of their research indicated that following participation in a treatment program, child pornography offenders admitted to a significantly greater number of sexual abuse crimes than before they were sentenced. Persons in this study group who had used the Internet to access child pornography were also significantly more likely to have committed a sexual contact crime. The authors conclude that persons using the Internet to commit child pornography offenses may also be undetected child molesters.

Need for Further Research and Changes in Approach to the Problem

Based on research conducted using various surveys, focus-group studies, and other data compilations, the authors of the studies reviewed in this bibliography made several recommendations regarding the need for additional research in the area of Internet crimes against children. In addition, they suggest ways in which parents, educators, and law enforcement officials can gain greater awareness of the magnitude of this problem, and consequently be better able to stem the proliferation of sexually explicit material through the Internet. Many of the recommendations specifically directed to parents are discussed above in the section "Role of the Family and Other Caregivers."

Ybarra and Mitchell, analyzing data from the first (2000) youth survey, identified several areas warranting further research: the small group of females intentionally seeking pornography; the link between purposeful exposure to pornography and emotional challenges, such as major depression or a poor emotional bond with a caregiver; the role of alcohol in delinquent behavior involving intentional seeking of pornography; and whether or not the Internet has become a more common mode of intentional exposure to pornography among adolescents than the viewing of sexually explicit material offline. Mitchell, Finkelhor, and Wolak, in "Online Requests for Sexual Pictures from Youth," recommend that pediatric and adolescent health professionals be aware of the incidence of online requests for sexual pictures of youths and of the Internet's role in expanding the production of child pornography. These same authors, in their study "Trends in Youth Reports of Sexual Solicitations, Harassment and Unwanted Exposure to Pornography on the Internet," recommend that caregivers, social service providers, and law enforcement agents target minority and less affluent populations for prevention programs, to protect them from online harassment and from predators. In their study of Internet-initiated sex crimes against minors, these authors acknowledge that Internet victim-prevention programs have emphasized the dangers of predator deception but find that educators fail to address the problems of young persons who are befriended by adult predators online and willingly meet with them to have voluntary sexual relationships. In another study using data extrapolated from the first (2000) youth survey, these authors concluded that a major flaw in the 2000 study—the lack of standardized, validated procedures for collecting data on children exposed to sexual material on the Internet—indicated the urgent need to collect further evidence to inform public policy aimed at protecting youth from unwanted exposure to Internet pornography.

Sources for Annotated Bibliography Executive Summary

Berson, Ilene R. "Grooming Cybervictims: The Psychological Effects of Online Exploitation for Youth." *Journal of School Violence* 2, no. 1 (2003): 9–18. http://www.cs.auckland.ac.nz/~john/NetSafe/I.Berson.pdf (accessed March 20, 2009).

Bourke, Michael L., and Andres E. Hernandez. "The 'Butner Study' Redux: A Report of the Incidence of Hands-on Child Victimization by Child Pornography Offenders." *Journal of Family Violence* 24, no. 3 (April 2009): 183–93.

Brown, Duncan. "Developing Strategies for Collecting and Presenting Grooming Evidence in a High Tech World." *Update* (National Center for Prosecution of Child Abuse), 2001, 1. http:www.ndaa.org/publications/newsletters/update_volume_14_number_11_2001.html (accessed March 24, 2009).

Cameron, Kenzie A., and Laura F. Salazar. "Adolescents' Experience with Sex on the Web: Results from Online Focus Groups." *Journal of Adolescence* 28, no. 4 (2005): 535–40.

Cho, Chang-Hoan, and Hongsik John Cheon. "Children's Exposure to Negative Internet Content: Effects of Family Context." *Journal of Broadcasting and Electronic Media* 49, no. 4 (December 2005). http://findarticles.com/p/articles/mi_m6836/is_4_49/ai_n25120984/ (accessed May 2009).

Dombrowski, Stefan C., Karen L. Gischlar, and Theo Durst. "Safeguarding Young People from Cyber Pornography and Cyber Sexual Predation: A Major Dilemma of the Internet." *Child Abuse Review* 16, no. 3 (2007): 153–70.

Greenfield, Patricia M. "Inadvertent Exposure to Pornography on the Internet: Implications of Peer-to-Peer File-Sharing Networks for Child Development and Families." *Applied Developmental Psychology* 25 (2004): 741–50.

Huang, Wilson, Mathew Earl Leopard, and Andrea Brockman. "Internet Child Sexual Exploitation: Offenses, Offenders, and Victims." In *Crimes of the Internet*, edited by Frank Schmalleger and Michael Pittaro, 43–65. Upper Saddle River, NJ: Pearson Education, 2009.

Internet Safety Technical Task Force. "Enhancing Child Safety and Online Technologies: Final Report of the Internet Safety Technical Task Force to the Multi-State Working Group on Social Networking of State Attorneys General of the United States." Report, Internet Safety Technical Task Force, Berkman Center for Internet and Society, Harvard University, Cambridge, MA, December 31, 2008. http://cyber.law.harvard.edu/pubrelease/isttf/ (accessed January 5, 2009).

Kowalski, Robin M., and Susan P. Limber. "Electronic Bullying Among Middle School Students." *Journal of Adolescent Health* 41, no. 6 (2007): S22–S30. http://www.wct-law.com/CM/Custom/Electronic%20Bullying%20Among%20Middle%20School%20Students.pdf (accessed March 24, 2009).

Lenhart, Amanda. "Cyberbullying and Online Teens." Research Memo, Pew/Internet and American Life Project, Pew Research Center, Washington, DC, June 27, 2007. http://www.pewinternet.org/~/media//Files/Reports/2007/PIP%20Cyberbullying%20Memo.pdf.pdf (accessed March 23, 2009).

Malamuth, Neil, and Mark Huppin. "Drawing the Line on Virtual Child Pornography: Bringing the Law in Line with the Research Evidence." *New York University Review of Law and Social Change* 31 (2006–2007): 773–827.

McQuade, Samuel C., III, and Neel Sampat. "Survey of Internet and At-Risk Behaviors: Undertaken by School Districts of Monroe County, New York, May 2007 to June 2008 and October 2007 to January 2008." Report, Center for Multidisciplinary Studies, Rochester Institute of Technology, Rochester, New York, June 18, 2008.

Moessner, Chris. "Cyberbullying." *Trends and Tudes*, April 2007, 1–4. http://www.harrisinteractive.com/news/newsletters/k12news/HI_TrendsTudes_2007_v06_i04.pdf (accessed March 23, 2009).

Mitchell, Kimberly J., David Finkelhor, and Janis Wolak. "Online Requests for Sexual Pictures from Youth: Risk Factors and Incident Characteristics." *Journal of Adolescent Health* 41, no. 2 (2007): 196–203. http://www.unh.edu/ccrc/pdf/CV155.pdf (accessed March 27, 2009).

Mitchell, Kimberly J., David Finkelhor, and Janis Wolak. "Victimization of Youths on the Internet." *Journal of Aggression, Maltreatment and Trauma* 8, nos. 1–2 (May 2003): 1–39.

Mitchell, Kimberly J., Janis Wolak, and David Finkelhor. "Police Posing as Juveniles Online to Catch Sex Offenders: Is It Working?" *Sexual Abuse: A Journal of Research and Treatment* 17, no. 3 (July 2005): 241–67. http://www.unh.edu/ccrc/pdf/CV82.pdf (accessed March 28, 2009).

Mitchell, Kimberly J., Janis Wolak, and David Finkelhor. "Trends in Youth Reports of Sexual Solicitations, Harassment and Unwanted Exposure to Pornography on the Internet." *Journal of Adolescent Health* 40, no. 2 (2007): 116–26. http://www.unh.edu/ccrc/pdf/CV135.pdf (accessed March 24, 2009).

Roban, Whitney. "The Net Effect: Girls and New Media." Executive Summary, Girl Scout Research Institute, Girl Scouts of the United States of America, New York, 2002. http://www.girlscouts.org/research/pdf/net_effect.pdf (accessed March 20, 2009).

Sabina, Chiara, Janis Wolak, and David Finkelhor. "Rapid Communication: The Nature and Dynamics of Internet Pornography Exposure for Youth." *CyberPsychology and Behavior* 11, no. 6 (2008): 691–93.

Strom, Paris S., and Robert D. Strom. "Cyberbullying by Adolescents: A Preliminary Assessment." *Educational Forum* 70, no. 1 (Fall 2005): 21–36.

U.S. Congress. House of Representatives. Committee on Energy and Commerce. Subcommittee on Oversight and Investigations. "Sexual Exploitation of Children over the Internet." 109th Cong., 2d sess., January 2007. Staff Report. http://republicans.energycommerce.house.gove/108/News/01032007_Report.pdf (accessed May 2009).

U. S. General Accounting Office. "File-Sharing Programs: Peer-to-Peer Networks Provide Ready Access to Child Pornography." Report to the Chairman and Ranking Minority Member, Committee on Government Reform, House of Representatives, no. GAO–03–351, Washington, DC, 2003.

Wells, Melissa, David Finkelhor, Janis Wolak, and Kimberly J. Mitchell. "Defining Child Pornography: Law Enforcement Dilemmas in Investigations of Internet Child Pornography Possession." *Police Practice and Research* 8, no. 3 (July 2007): 269–82.

Wolak, Janis, David Finkelhor, and Kimberly J. Mitchell. "Internet-Initiated Sex Crimes Against Minors: Implications for Prevention Based on Findings from a National Study." *Journal of Adolescent Health* 35, no. 5 (2004): 11–20. http://www.unh.edu/ccrc/pdf/CV71.pdf (accessed March 23, 2009).

Wolak, Janis, Kimberly J. Mitchell, and David Finkelhor. "Unwanted and Wanted Exposure to Online Pornography in a National Sample of Youth Internet Users." *Pediatrics* 119, no. 2 (2007): 247–57.

Ybarra, Michele L., and Kimberly J. Mitchell. "Exposure to Internet Pornography among Children and Adolescents: A National Survey." *CyberPsychology and Behavior* 8, no. 5 (2005): 473–86.

Ybarra, Michele L., and Kimberly J. Mitchell. "Prevalence and Frequency of Internet Harassment Instigation: Implications for Adolescent Health." *Journal of Adolescent Health* 41, no. 2 (2007): 189–95. http://www.unh.edu/ccrc/pdf/CV157.pdf (accessed March 20, 2009).

ANNOTATED BIBLIOGRAPHY

Child Pornography/Exposure to Sexually Explicit Material

Bourke, Michael L., and Andres E. Hernandez. "The 'Butner Study' Redux: A Report of the Incidence of Hands-on Child Victimization by Child Pornography Offenders." *Journal of Family Violence* 24, no. 3 (April 2009): 183–93.

The study sought to determine whether a person who viewed and/or collected child pornography was at low risk of committing a sexual contact crime against a child, or if such a person is a contact sex offender whose crimes have gone undetected. The study consisted of two analyses. In the first analysis, the authors examined information about offenders' criminal sexual histories collected prior to and following participation in a treatment program. Following treatment, offenders admitting to contact crimes increased from 26 percent to 85 percent, and the average number of victims per offender increased from 1.88 to 13.56. The second analysis examined only the subset of offenders acknowledging at the end of treatment that they had committed at least one contact crime against a child. The results showed an increase across all categories compared to what was known at the time of sentencing: the number of offenders acknowledging abuse of both pre- and post-pubescent victims increased 47 percent; those admitting to have victimized both males and females increased from 15 to 40 percent; and among offenders without any known victims at the time of sentencing, 24 percent acknowledged victims of both genders, and 48 percent admitted to contact crimes against pre- and post-pubescent victims. The authors also found that persons in this sample group who had used the Internet to access child pornography were significantly more likely to have committed a contact crime. From this result, they concluded that this population of offenders may also be undetected child molesters.

Huang, Wilson, Mathew Earl Leopard, and Andrea Brockman. "Internet Child Sexual Exploitation: Offenses, Offenders, and Victims." In *Crimes of the Internet*, edited by Frank Schmalleger and Michael Pittaro, 43–65. Upper Saddle River, NJ: Pearson Education, 2009.

The authors of this chapter in a book about various Internet crimes discuss factors contributing to the rapid growth of online sexual exploitation of children, linking it to increased Internet accessibility and anonymity, commercialization of exploitative media, and digitization in the production and dissemination of images. The authors found that, despite legislative initiatives intended to keep pace with the incidence of this type of crime against children, the nature and distribution of child pornography, as well as the characteristics of offenders and victims alike, have remained similar over time and across a wide sample of studies. The chapter includes an overview of legislative developments and case law in this area, including the various legal definitions of what constitutes child pornography. The authors discuss types of images of child abuse, distinguishing between images, pornography, and erotica produced commercially and those that are homemade. Homemade images, although never produced for commercial profit, circulate repeatedly in the pedophile community, forming a substantial portion of currently circulating images. The authors compare the findings of numerous recent studies, discussing the behavior of perpetrators, the reasons they collect images of child abuse, the personal characteristics of individuals who produce and collect child pornography, and the personal characteristics of their victims. Finally, the authors highlight new federal legislation, as well as new Internet developments, noting problems that have arisen with the use of social-networking sites like My Space and the use of webcams and similar technologies that blend the roles of the producer and the victim of child pornography.

Internet Safety Technical Task Force. "Enhancing Child Safety and Online Technologies: Final Report of the Internet Safety Technical Task Force to the Multi-State Working Group on Social Networking of State Attorneys General of the United States." Report, Internet Safety Technical Task Force, Berkman Center for Internet and Society, Harvard University, Cambridge, MA, December 31, 2008. http://cyber.law.harvard.edu/pubrelease/isttf/ (accessed January 5, 2009).

In this final report, the Internet Safety Technical Task Force summarizes and analyzes two previous documents produced by the Task Force—a literature review of relevant research about the online safety of youth in the United States and a review of 40 technologies intended to increase online safety. The Task Force also analyzes the efforts of eight leading social-networking sites to enhance the online safety of minors and makes recommendations concerning the best methods of ensuring the online safety of youth. The Task Force's literature review revealed that, although the risks facing youth online are complex, they are not significantly different from the risks facing youth offline. Moreover, the Task Force found that, as minors get older, they themselves contribute to the problem of online safety. Regarding the 40 technologies intended to enhance Internet safety, the Task Force recommends that caregivers and law enforcement agencies should carefully weigh the privacy and security issues associated with these technologies against their potential benefits.

Overall, the Task Force concludes that no single technological solution or specific combination of technological solutions can solve the problem of online safety for minors; rather, adults must employ these technologies in concert with other methods, including parental oversight, education, social services, and law enforcement. In addition, the Task Force recommends that social-networking sites and service providers should enact sound policies to protect minors from online predators.

McQuade, Samuel C., III, and Neel Sampat. "Survey of Internet and At-Risk Behaviors: Undertaken by School Districts of Monroe County, New York, May 2007 to June 2008 and October 2007 to January 2008." Report, Center for Multidisciplinary Studies, Rochester Institute of Technology, Rochester, New York, June 18, 2008.

In partnership with 14 school districts, the Rochester Institute of Technology (RIT) carried out a major study in 2007, which included an online survey of more than 40,000 students. The study measured the nature and extent of online experiences, as offender or as victim, of students in kindergarten through twelfth grade; determined levels and types of parental supervision over children's use of computers and portable electronic devices; and obtained information from teachers regarding their perceptions of school-related cyber abuse and crime. The surveys targeted students in developmentally distinct age and grade levels, as well as the parents of the students and the teachers and staff of their schools.

The results of the study indicate that children begin using the Internet at kindergarten age or younger and that online activities of children in grades K–12 include inappropriate behavior and exposure to inappropriate content. Cyberbullying and victimization begins as early as second grade for some children, and by middle school, students as a group experience or engage in all known forms of cyber abuse and online aggression. Online exchange of sexually explicit content typically begins in middle school. The study results also report that students consistently say that they are less supervised than their parents say that they are: 66 percent of high school students reported that their parents provide no supervision of Internet activities, but only 7 percent of parents reported that they do not provide any supervision.

Sabina, Chiara, Janis Wolak, and David Finkelhor. "Rapid Communication: The Nature and Dynamics of Internet Pornography Exposure for Youth." *CyberPsychology and Behavior* 11, no. 6 (2008): 691–93.

The article reports the results of a 2006 online survey in which researchers questioned a sample of college students about their exposure to online pornography before the age of 18, comparing the responses of male and female students. In the final sample of 563 students, 72.8 percent (93.2 percent of the male students and 62.1 percent of the female students) reported that they had viewed online pornography before the age of 18. Most initial exposure had occurred between the ages of 14 and 17, with boys significantly more likely to view pornography frequently and to view a variety of images and girls significantly more likely to expose themselves to pornography involuntarily. Specifically, 6.8 percent of males reported that they had never purposely sought exposure to pornography, whereas 42.3 percent of females reported that they had never looked for pornography on purpose. A small minority of the students reported that viewing online pornography before the age of 18 had strongly affected their attitudes or emotions about sexuality. Of this group, boys were more likely to report feeling excitement, whereas girls were more likely to experience embarrassment and disgust. However, the researchers found considerable diversity in the extent of and reactions to online pornography, and, therefore, suggested that relying on gender stereotypes might obscure the full picture of how youth respond to exposure.

Wells, Melissa, David Finkelhor, Janis Wolak, and Kimberly J. Mitchell. "Defining Child Pornography: Law Enforcement Dilemmas in Investigations of Internet Child Pornography Possession." *Police Practice and Research* 8, no. 3 (July 2007): 269–82.

The authors examine law enforcement agencies' difficulty defining child pornography, using a sample of 34 cases of reported possession of Internet child pornography in which law enforcement officers had made no arrest. Researchers analyzed data collected as part of the National Juvenile Online Victimization (NJOV) Study. NJOV sought to capture estimates of the incidence of Internet sex crimes against minors occurring during the course of one year (2000–2001), which had come to the attention of law enforcement officials. In addition, NJOV attempted to identify problems in the investigations of those crimes. Analysts' findings reflected two dilemmas facing law enforcement agencies that can prevent their making an arrest in a child pornography case: 1) the nature of the child pornography portrayed in the confiscated images may not fit the definitions of existing statutes and 2) investigators may not be able to determine the age of the children in the images with certainty.

Wolak, Janis, Kimberly J. Mitchell, and David Finkelhor. "Unwanted and Wanted Exposure to Online Pornography in a National Sample of Youth Internet Users." *Pediatrics* 119, no. 2 (2007): 247–57.

The Crimes Against Children Research Center at the University of New Hampshire designed the Youth Internet Safety Survey to determine the incidence of and risk factors for youth exposure to sexual content on the Internet. In the Second Youth Internet Safety Survey, the researchers conducted a telephone survey between March and June 2005, interviewing a nationally representative sample of 1,500 youth Internet users ages 10 to 17. In this article, based on the analysis of the data from that survey, the researchers report the extent of both wanted and unwanted exposure to online pornography among regular Internet users in that age-group and assess associated risk factors. The researchers found that 42 percent of youth Internet users (approximately 600) had viewed online pornography during the previous year. Of that 42 percent, 66 percent of the youth (approximately 400) reported that they had not sought or desired the exposure to pornography. Thirty-four percent of youth Internet users viewing pornography online reported a mixture of intentional exposure only or both wanted and unwanted exposure during 2005, up from 25 percent during 1999 and 2000. The youth reported that unwanted exposure had occurred only during a single Internet activity—when they were using file-sharing programs to download images.

U.S. Congress. House of Representatives. Committee on Energy and Commerce. Subcommittee on Oversight and Investigations. "Sexual Exploitation of Children over the Internet." 109th Cong., 2d sess., January 2007. Staff Report. http://republicans.energycommerce.house.gove/108/News/01032007_Report.pdf (accessed May 2009).

Prompted by Kurt Eichenwald's article, "Through His Webcam, a Boy Joins a Sordid Online World," which appeared in the *New York Times* at the end of 2005, the House Energy and Commerce Subcommittee on Oversight and Investigations studied the United States' efforts to curb the sexual exploitation of children over the Internet. Committee staff investigated the information Eichenwald had reported; visited federal law enforcement agency offices and conducted interviews; reviewed and analyzed existing federal law with regard to criminal penalties for possession, creation, and distribution of child pornography; and held hearings from April through September 2006.

The subcommittee reports that the ease of trading, selling, and downloading pornographic images of children from the Internet contributes to the increased incidence of sexual exploitation of children in the United States and the world. The number of sexually exploitative images of children on the Internet is increasing, and victims are typically younger and the images more violent than in the past. Commercially available child pornography on the Internet may comprise a multibillion-dollar-per-year industry. Although law enforcement agencies at the state level prosecute 70 percent of all cases involving sexual exploitation of children over the Internet, the subcommittee found a wide discrepancy among state criminal codes in their treatment of these offenses and in their sentencing practices. Investigators also reported that encryption methods, such as anonymizers, significantly interfere with law enforcement's ability to investigate and bring charges against offenders. The subcommittee also found that Web sites hosted in the United States appear to account for more than half of the child pornography on the Internet.

Malamuth, Neil, and Mark Huppin. "Drawing the Line on Virtual Child Pornography: Bringing the Law in Line with the Research Evidence." *New York University Review of Law and Social Change* 31 (2006–2007): 773–827.

This New York University law review article seeks to determine whether documented incidences of the use of various kinds of child pornography may be used as evidentiary material in child molestation cases. The authors used scientific literature to identify those individuals who might have a risk factor for perpetrating sexually abusive acts after exposure to virtual child pornography and attempted to assess the degree of risk such exposure might create for persons with this predisposition.

Drawing a clear distinction between pedophiles (individuals who are sexually aroused by children) and child molesters (individuals who commit sexual acts against children), the authors reviewed various case studies and found that, whereas child molesters use pornography to groom potential victims, as well as to self-stimulate before committing a sex crime against a child, pedophiles are less likely to molest a child after viewing pornography. A minority reported that pedophiles are more likely to molest a child after viewing pornography. The authors also analyzed scientific literature on aggression and on pornography that portrays nonconsenting adults, attempting to draw links among risk factors, exposure to child pornography, and the likelihood of a person committing a contact crime against a child. The authors conclude that whether exposure to real or virtual child pornography affects a person's behavior depends on a number of risk factors, and that, therefore, no strong causal relationship exists between viewing child pornography and committing sexual molestation of a child.

Cho, Chang-Hoan, and Hongsik John Cheon. "Children's Exposure to Negative Internet Content: Effects of Family Context." *Journal of Broadcasting and Electronic Media* 49, no. 4 (December 2005). http://findarticles.com/p/articles/mi_m6836/is_4_49/ai_n25120984/ (accessed May 2009).

The article reports the results of an extensive review of the literature and a survey of 190 families, which the researchers conducted to study the extent of children's exposure to negative Internet content including pornography, violence, and sexual solicitation. The researchers simultaneously examined the discrepancy between parents' perception of their children's Internet use and their children's actual activities. The primary focus of this study was the social context of children's Internet use, particularly the relationship of their Internet use to family dynamics. The researchers believe that, rather than merely reporting the children's visits to Web sites or their general online activities, this study contributes new data concerning the content that children actually encounter on the Internet. In addition, the study provides new information regarding the role that the family environment and parent–child relationship play in a child's exposure to negative Internet content. Moreover, the authors believe that their research contributes a theoretical framework that encompasses both the incidence of children's negative exposure online and parents' perceived control over their children's Internet activities.

The researchers found that parents generally underestimate their children's exposure to negative material on the Internet. They suggest that, in fact, children encounter negative content more frequently than their parents believe. The study agrees with research conducted prior to 1995 that examined the effects of family communication patterns on children's use of mass media—finding that as with earlier studies, parents of families exhibiting high levels of cohesion perceive greater control over and understanding of their children's Internet use.

Ybarra, Michele L., and Kimberly J. Mitchell. "Exposure to Internet Pornography among Children and Adolescents: A National Survey." *CyberPsychology and Behavior* 8, no. 5 (2005): 473–86.

Analyzing data from the First Youth Internet Safety Survey (2000), which the Crimes Against Children Research Center at the University of New Hampshire designed to determine the incidence of and risk factors for youth exposure to sexual content on the Internet, this study focuses on youth who intentionally seek pornography. The authors found that the majority of youth who reported seeking pornography online and offline were male; only 5 percent of females reported having looked for pornography. The majority (87 percent) of those who reported having sought sexual images online were older than 14. The authors of the study noted the developmental appropriateness of this curiosity about sexuality in youth over the age of 14. The survey measured the following: pornography seeking, demographic characteristics, Internet-usage characteristics, unwanted exposure to sexual material, parental Internet controls, caregiver–child relationships, and psychosocial characteristics. The authors found that, although the majority of youth intentionally seeking pornography online are older than 14, younger children reported exposure to sexual images in magazines or on television. The younger children who were regular Internet users and who reported that they had intentionally sought pornography also reported a significantly higher incidence of delinquent behavior, substance use, or clinical depression, or a combination of these.

Analysis of the data identified several areas warranting further research: the small group of females intentionally seeking pornography; the link between purposeful exposure to pornography and emotional challenges, such as major depression or a poor emotional bond with a caregiver; the role of alcohol in delinquent behavior involving intentional seeking of pornography; and whether or not the Internet has become a more common mode of intentional exposure to pornography among adolescents than the viewing of sexually explicit material offline.

Cameron, Kenzie A., and Laura F. Salazar. "Adolescents' Experience with Sex on the Web: Results from Online Focus Groups." *Journal of Adolescence* 28, no. 4 (2005): 535–40.

This study fills a gap in the data on the effects of online sexualized material on children and adolescents. The researchers recruited 40 adolescents—18 male and 22 female—ages 14 to 17 (in grades 9–11), who regularly used the Internet. The researchers divided the participants according to their age and gender into one of four Web-based focus groups. The focus-group interface among the participants in each group was similar to that in an online chat room, in which the participants are typically anonymous.

Focus-group participants reported having intentionally sought exposure to sexually oriented Web sites while searching for information related to sexual health or relationships. They reported having experienced unintentional exposure through personal e-mail with benign subject lines or when following misleading URLs. The participants reported an incidence of exposure to sexually explicit Web sites ranging from "never" to "daily," with most exposures occurring accidentally or unintentionally, via unsolicited e-mails containing explicit content or links to explicit material. Some participants reported having received 10 to 20 such e-mails per day. Most girls responded negatively to their exposure to sexually explicit material, and no girls reported intentional exposure. A subgroup of boys reported intentional exposure, whereas some reported that they had not sought to view the sexual content, stating that they considered explicit material "sick." Both boys and girls reported their perception that exposure to sexually explicit material had no effect on their personal views of either gender or of relationships. The authors of the study suggested further research in this area, noting that this perception contradicts previous research documenting the negative effects of adolescents' exposure to sexually explicit content.

Cooper, Sharon, Richard J. Estes, Angelo P. Giardino, Nancy D. Kellog, and Victor I. Vieth, eds. *Medical, Legal, and Social Science Aspects of Child Sexual Exploitation: A Comprehensive Review of Pornography, Prostitution, and Internet Crimes*. 2 vols. St. Louis, MO: G.W. Medical Publishing, 2005.

This two-volume set provides a repository of information for multidisciplinary teams studying Internet crimes against children. Volume 1 offers an overview of the scope of the problem of sexual exploitation of children, covering the subjects of pornography and online solicitation. Survivors, including prostituted children and youth, report their experiences. Chapters in volume 1 discuss abusive images of children on the Internet, the commercial sexual exploitation of children in North America, methods Internet predators use to exploit children sexually, and young people's remarks about online victimization. Volume 2 addresses the investigation and prosecution of Internet crimes against children and makes recommendations on how to prevent the exploitation of children. Topics in volume 2 include important actors in the investigation process, such as the U.S. Postal Inspection Service and first responders; the investigation process itself; issues concerning prosecution of purveyors of child pornography; the criminal justice system—including perspectives of victims, juvenile courts, and judges; pedophiles' activities on the Internet; and computer forensic software.

Greenfield, Patricia M. "Inadvertent Exposure to Pornography on the Internet: Implications of Peer-to-Peer File-Sharing Networks for Child Development and Families." *Applied Developmental Psychology* 25 (2004): 741–50.

In this article, Patricia M. Greenfield of the Children's Medical Center and the Department of Psychology of the University of California at Los Angeles reports her March 13, 2003, testimony before the House Committee on Government Reform regarding the risk of children's and adolescents' unintended exposure to pornography through peer-to-peer file-sharing networks. In her testimony, Greenfield responded to the committee's questions concerning the developmental effects on children of exposure to pornography through file-sharing networks; the challenges parents face in limiting children's access to pornography online; and nontechnical tools available to parents that can help them address these challenges.

Greenfield provided overviews of various research studies and their findings. She concluded that evidence supports the thesis that pornography and sexualized material can influence the moral values, sexual activity, and sexual attitudes of children and youth, including their attitudes toward sexual violence; that peer-to-peer file-sharing networks are part of a pervasive, sexualized media environment that leads to inadvertent exposure of children and youth to pornography and other adult sexual content; and that a warm, communicative parent–child relationship, appropriate sex education, and parental participation in children's Internet activities are critical factors in protecting children from adverse effects of exposure to explicit sexual material. Greenfield also stated that parents of boys at risk for antisocial behavior should monitor their sons' Internet use carefully and limit their access to online pornography.

Mitchell, Kimberly J., David Finkelhor, and Janis Wolak. "Victimization of Youths on the Internet." *Journal of Aggression, Maltreatment and Trauma* 8, nos. 1–2 (May 2003): 1–39.

The Crimes Against Children Research Center at the University of New Hampshire designed the Youth Internet Safety Survey to determine the incidence of and risk factors for youth exposure to sexual content on the Internet. The First Youth Internet Safety Survey (2000) surveyed a nationally representative sample of 1,500 youth, examining the dangers that children and adolescents face when communicating, gathering information, or seeking entertainment on the Internet. The survey asked participants about unwanted sexual solicitations, unwanted exposure to sexual material, and online harassment during the previous year. In this article, researchers report their analysis of data from the survey.

The authors found that predators had targeted girls for sexual solicitation at almost twice the rate of boys, and youth who were at least 15 years old accounted for nearly two-thirds of incidents of unwanted exposure. In instances of harassment, predators had targeted boys and girls equally. The survey revealed that adults were responsible for 24 percent of solicitations—most of those adults were ages 18 to 25; only 4 percent of those soliciting were older than 25. Juveniles accounted for nearly half of all those targeted and for half of all aggressive solicitations. Harassment caused the young people the most distress—they described 31 percent of the instances of harassment as extremely upsetting, while 20 percent reported extremely upsetting solicitations, and 23 percent of youth felt extremely upset when exposed to sexual material. The authors found that young people at risk for unwanted solicitation, harassment, and exposure to sexual content on the Internet tend to be troubled, older adolescents who use the Internet frequently and engage in high-risk online behavior. However, they also found that half of the youth reporting unwanted solicitation, harassment, or exposure to sexual materials were not troubled, high-rate Internet users or frequent online risk takers.

Mitchell, Kimberly J., David Finkelhor, and Janis Wolak. "The Exposure of Youth to Unwanted Sexual Material on the Internet: A National Survey of Risk, Impact, and Prevention." *Youth and Society* 34, no. 3 (March 2003): 330–58.

Analyzing data from the First Youth Internet Safety Survey (2000), which the Crimes Against Children Research Center at the University of New Hampshire designed to determine the incidence of and risk factors for youth exposure to sexual material on the Internet, the researchers sought to identify a subset of unwanted exposure described as very or extremely distressing. Twenty-four percent of the 1,500 youth surveyed in this nationally representative sample reported feeling very or extremely upset about exposure to sexually explicit material, 21 percent reported feeling very or extremely embarrassed, and 19 percent reported experiencing at least one stress symptom related to the episode. Youth reporting symptoms of stress said that they had stayed away from the Internet after the incident, could not stop thinking about the episode, felt jumpy or irritable, or had lost interest in their usual pursuits. In 43 percent of the episodes, the youth had not disclosed their exposure to anybody. Those that did report it usually told a parent, friend, or sibling. When the youth or their family reported the incident to an authority, they most frequently told a teacher or school official or the Internet service provider, but they had never reported the incident to police.

The authors of the study discussed the survey's flaws, such as the lack of standardized, validated procedures for collecting data on children exposed to sexual material on the Internet. They conclude that the study indicates the urgent need to collect further evidence to inform public policy aimed at protecting youth from unsought exposure to sexually explicit material on the Internet.

U. S. General Accounting Office. "File-Sharing Programs: Peer-to-Peer Networks Provide Ready Access to Child Pornography." Report to the Chairman and Ranking Minority Member, Committee on Government Reform, House of Representatives, no. GAO–03–351, Washington, DC, 2003.

The U.S. General Accounting Office (GAO) produced this report in response to a request from the House Committee on Government Reform that GAO investigate the ease of access to child pornography on peer-to-peer networks; the risk of inadvertent exposure of juvenile users of peer-to-peer networks to pornography (including child pornography); and the extent of federal law enforcement resources for combating child pornography on peer-to-peer networks. Agents at the Customs Cyber-Smuggling Center performed searches, and GAO performed analyses based on keywords and file names only, finding that child pornography is easily found and downloaded from peer-to-peer networks. Depending on the keywords used, child pornography comprised between 42 and 44 percent of pornographic images found in a search of KaZaA (a popular peer-to-peer, file-sharing program). The results were consistent with the observations of the National Center for Missing and Exploited Children. Agents classified nearly half of the images downloaded from keyword searches using celebrity names and cartoon characters as pornography, indicating that youth face a significant risk of inadvertent exposure to pornography while using networks like KaZaA. GAO also analyzed data on the allocation of resources at four agencies, as well as resources that the National Center for Missing and Exploited Children had allocated to combat child pornography. GAO found that these agencies had not devoted significant resources to combating child exploitation and child pornography in 2003. GAO was unable to quantify the resources dedicated to child pornography investigations involving peer-to-peer networks.

Thornburgh, Dick, and Herbert S. Lin, eds. *Youth, Pornography and the Internet*. Washington, DC: National Academy Press, 2002.

This 450-page volume (including a bibliography and an index) is the product of a 1998 mandate of the U.S. Congress charging the National Research Council (NRC) to carry out a study of pornography on the Internet. In response, the NRC Computer Science and Telecommunications Board and the NRC Board on Children, Youth, and Families formed a committee to conduct the study. The committee members comprised a diverse group of people with expertise in constitutional law, law enforcement, libraries and library science, developmental and social psychology, information technologies, ethics, and education. Chapters in this volume cover relevant technologies, such as filtering, age verification software, and anonymizers; the adult online entertainment industry and its practices related to minors; legal and regulatory issues, particularly issues related to the First Amendment, to federal and state laws and regulatory efforts, and to law enforcement; children's exposure to sexually explicit material on the Internet; research concerning the effects on individuals of exposure to sexually explicit material; public debate concerning the effects of such exposure; and legal and regulatory tools for protecting children from obscene material on the Internet.

Jenkins, Philip. *Beyond Tolerance: Child Pornography on the Internet*. New York: New York University Press, 2001.

Over the course of nine chapters, Jenkins, a professor of history and religion who has written extensively about public perceptions of social problems, examines the issue of Internet regulation through the lens of child pornography. In the unique case of child pornography, Jenkins concludes that the government should impose some form of regulation aimed at drastically reducing the presence of child pornography on the Internet. However, he acknowledges the persistent difficulty of determining what law or laws might successfully achieve this end. Jenkins advocates the transformation of present law enforcement tactics and priorities to meet the goal of controlling child pornography. He explores society's views of child pornography and examines the new form of technology-driven social organization, which he considers responsible for perpetuating the problem of online child pornography.

In his discussion of the social context of online pornography, Jenkins provides an overview of the history of child pornography on the Internet and explains how the business of online child pornography developed, how it became highly organized and globalized, and why law enforcement officers have such difficulty identifying the participants. He examines the myths and realities of child pornography and discusses efforts to eradicate it, including debates about trade regulations, users' privacy, and individual rights; the official endeavors of law enforcement agencies; and the work of private activist groups.

Unwanted Sexual Solicitation

Dombrowski, Stefan C., Karen L. Gischlar, and Theo Durst. "Safeguarding Young People from Cyber Pornography and Cyber Sexual Predation: A Major Dilemma of the Internet." *Child Abuse Review* 16, no. 3 (2007): 153–70.

This article outlines technological and psychoeducational mechanisms to help caregivers—parents or guardians—protect children from online pornography and sexual solicitation. With the increased use of Internet technologies, such as e-mail, chat rooms, and peer-to-peer networks, children can easily connect with other people online at all times. Without caregiver supervision and interdiction of online communication, youth are vulnerable to exposure to pornography or to the solicitations of predators. However, the combination of technological methods and the vigilance of caregivers can deter solicitation and protect children from exposure to online pornography, safeguarding their emotional health. Software tools such as firewall security barriers, wireless encryption, antivirus protection, spyware detection and removal, and usage tracking help protect youth from accessing unsafe Web sites and allow the caregiver to review the child's online activity. However, although technological protections may stop some, determined predators can circumvent most of these methods. Therefore, caregivers also need to use psychoeducational measures, tailored to the child's developmental level, setting appropriate boundaries for online behavior.

Caregivers should discuss Internet dangers, supervise Internet friendships, monitor children's Internet use, and establish an Internet-use safety contract with the child. The article includes a sample Internet-use contract for the use of caregivers and their children. The authors prescribe a combination of technology-based tools and caregiver vigilance as the best way to defend children from solicitation and pornography.

Mitchell, Kimberly J., David Finkelhor, and Janis Wolak. "Online Requests for Sexual Pictures from Youth: Risk Factors and Incident Characteristics." *Journal of Adolescent Health* 41, no. 2 (2007): 196–203. http://www.unh.edu/ccrc/pdf/CV155.pdf (accessed March 27, 2009).

This study is based on data from the Second Youth Internet Safety Survey conducted between March and June 2005, in which researchers conducted telephone interviews with a nationally representative sample of 1,500 youth Internet users ages 10 to 17. The Crimes Against Children Research Center at the University of New Hampshire created the survey to examine youth exposure to sexual content on the Internet. The authors focus on one way that the Internet facilitates the production of child pornography: the solicitation of youth to produce sexually explicit images and to post or to transmit them online.

Reporting the demographic, psychological, and Internet-use characteristics of youth who received online solicitations for sexual pictures within the previous year, the authors found that 13 percent of youth in the study population had received unwanted sexual solicitations over the Internet, and 4 percent of the youth had received an online request to send a sexual picture of themselves. Only one youth out of the 65 who received such a request complied. Of the 1,500 survey respondents, 20 percent (300 youth) reported that they had received unwanted sexual solicitations or harassment, and 45 percent of those solicitations (136 youth—13 percent of the overall survey group) included requests for pictures. Forty-eight percent (65 youth) had received requests for sexual images. The survey found that youth who are female, black, in the presence of friends, have close online relationships, or engage in online sexual behavior are more likely than others to receive solicitations for sexual pictures. The study defined online relationships as relationships with peers and nonsexual relationships with adults, defining online sexual behavior as talking about sex online with someone the youth does not know personally. The authors call for pediatric and adolescent health professionals to be aware of the incidence of online requests for sexual pictures of youth and of the Internet's role in expanding the production of child pornography.

Mitchell, Kimberly J., Janis Wolak, and David Finkelhor. "Trends in Youth Reports of Sexual Solicitations, Harassment and Unwanted Exposure to Pornography on the Internet." *Journal of Adolescent Health* 40, no. 2 (2007): 116–26. http://www.unh.edu/ccrc/pdf/CV135.pdf (accessed March 24, 2009).

This 2007 report compares the results of two surveys, designed by the Crimes Against Children Research Center at the University of New Hampshire and conducted in 2000 and 2005, regarding unwanted sexual solicitation, harassment, and exposure to pornography on the Internet. In the First and Second Youth Internet Safety Surveys, researchers conducted telephone interviews with a nationally representative sample of youth Internet users ages 10 to 17. This article differentiates the results of the two surveys according to demographic characteristics, such as age, gender, race, and household income, revealing changes that occurred between 2000 and 2005. The surveys defined unwanted sexual solicitations as requests to engage in sexual activities or sexual talk, or as adults' requests for sexual information from a juvenile; they defined online harassment as threats or other aggressive behavior toward a youth, sent or posted online; and they defined unwanted exposure to pornography as unsought and unexpected exposure to pictures of naked people or of people having sex.

In general, the results of the two surveys indicated that, although unwanted sexual solicitations had declined, online harassment and unwanted exposure to pornography had increased between 2000 and 2005. Unwanted sexual solicitations had decreased, overall, from 19 percent to 13 percent. The decline in such activity was most apparent among white youth living in affluent areas. However, the incidence of online harassment had risen from 6 percent to 9 percent overall, and the incidence of unwanted exposure to pornography had risen from 25 percent to 34 percent. Demographic subgroups showed different results for the incidence of sexual solicitation and unwanted exposure to pornography. For example, the 2005 survey showed that black youth and low-income families had experienced an increased incidence of sexual solicitation. Unwanted exposure to pornography had increased among youth 10 to 12 years old, 16- to 17-year olds, boys, and white, non-Hispanic youth. The authors observe that, despite the decline in certain types of Internet crimes against children, young people continue to experience offensive episodes online. Caregivers, social service providers, and law enforcement agents need to target minority and less affluent populations for prevention programs, to protect them from online harassment and from predators.

Mitchell, Kimberly J., Janis Wolak, and David Finkelhor. "Police Posing as Juveniles Online to Catch Sex Offenders: Is It Working?" *Sexual Abuse: A Journal of Research and Treatment* 17, no. 3 (July 2005): 241–67. http://www.unh.edu/ccrc/pdf/CV82.pdf (accessed March 28, 2009).

The article explores the extent and effectiveness of proactive online investigations, in which police investigators use the Internet—posing as minors and often assuming a different gender—to communicate via chat rooms, e-mail, and instant messaging, to interdict youth enticement and child pornography. The authors used data from the National Juvenile Online Victimization Study (NJOV), which reported characteristics of Internet sex crimes against minors, to create a survey for law enforcement agencies. The survey of 2,574 state, county, and local law enforcement agencies found that, through proactive investigations, the agencies had made 124 arrests for Internet sex crimes against children during the year beginning July 1, 2000, and ending June 30, 2001.

The authors found that a significant proportion—25 percent—of all arrests for Internet crimes against children were the outcome of proactive investigations. Proactive investigations resulted in offenders entering pleas 91 percent of the time and going to trial 15 percent of the time (some offenders had multiple charges, accounting for the discrepancy in the percentages). Investigators most frequently posed as girls of 12 years old or older, meeting targeted predators in chat rooms or through instant messaging. In 87 percent of the cases, investigators conducted their investigations using multiple forms of online communication. The authors point out that, in 63 percent of the cases reviewed, the law enforcement agency had received no federal funding for this kind of investigative work. They conclude that, because of the high rate of arrest and the potential to stop a perpetrator before a child is molested, law enforcement agencies should continue to conduct proactive investigations.

Wolak, Janis, David Finkelhor, and Kimberly J. Mitchell. "Internet-Initiated Sex Crimes Against Minors: Implications for Prevention Based on Findings from a National Study." *Journal of Adolescent Health* 35, no. 5 (2004): 11–20. http://www.unh.edu/ccrc/pdf/CV71.pdf (accessed March 23, 2009).

This article describes characteristics of interactions between Internet predators and their juvenile victims. Survey results revealed that the majority of victims had met the predator willingly. In a mailed survey and follow-up telephone interview with law enforcement investigators, conducted between October 2001 and July 2002, researchers identified 129 Internet-initiated sex crimes. The cases involved sex-crime victims, ages 17 and younger, who had first met the predator on the Internet. Face-to-face meetings had occurred in 74 percent of the cases, and 93 percent of those encounters had included sexual contact. Most of the victims (73 percent) met with the predators more than once. The majority of victims (67 percent) were children between the ages of 12 and 15, and 75 percent of the victims were girls. The most common first encounter of a predator with a victim took place in an online chat room (76 percent). In 47 percent of the cases, the predator offered gifts or money during the relationship-building phase.

This study found that two widely held beliefs regarding online predation were incorrect. First, the researchers found that predators use less deception to befriend their online victims than experts had thought. Only 5 percent of the predators told their victims that they were in the same age-group as the victim. Most offenders told the victim that they were older males seeking sexual relations. Second, a large majority of the victims who responded to this survey had willingly met and had sexual encounters with the predators. Internet victim-prevention programs have emphasized the dangers of predator deception, but, thus far, educators have not addressed the problems of youth who are willing to meet with adults to have voluntary sexual relationships. The authors conclude that vulnerable youth need further education regarding the negative effects of such relationships.

Berson, Ilene R. "Grooming Cybervictims: The Psychological Effects of Online Exploitation for Youth." *Journal of School Violence* 2, no. 1 (2003): 9–18. http://www.cs.auckland.ac.nz/~john/NetSafe/I.Berson.pdf (accessed March 20, 2009).

This article describes how online predators prepare potential child victims for abuse. The Internet poses a challenge for young users, because children's naïveté and trust make them vulnerable targets for predators seeking to groom them for illicit activities. In addition, the Internet permits anonymity, enabling the predator to hide his or her age and gender from the victim. Victims are often too young to interpret cues that would make an older person cautious.

Predators manipulate their victims through a process known as grooming, using techniques to lower the child's inhibitions and build his or her trust in the predator. Young people share personal information in chat rooms or in e-mail, not realizing that predators use such information to develop victim profiles, build an online friendship, and gain trust. The predator preys upon a child's loneliness and emotional neediness, gradually increasing the intensity of the interaction with the child by offering attention, friendship, and gifts. After building the child's trust, the perpetrator may gradually expose the child to pornography to lower the child's inhibitions, desensitize the child to nudity, and validate adult–child sexual relations. Finally, the perpetrator requests a personal meeting with the victim. Parents, schools, and government agencies need to foster awareness of online exploitation, explain to children the lures that predators offer them, and teach them to discriminate among types of online interactions, including ambiguous chat or e-mail content and potentially threatening exchanges.

Brown, Duncan. "Developing Strategies for Collecting and Presenting Grooming Evidence in a High Tech World." *Update* (National Center for Prosecution of Child Abuse), 2001, 1. http:www.ndaa.org/publications/newsletters/update_volume_14_number_11_2001.html (accessed March 24, 2009).

In this unique article, a guide for prosecutors seeking to prosecute online predators, the author describes the process that online predators use to prepare children for sexual exploitation—a process known as grooming —explaining the type of evidence against predators that law enforcement officers need to acquire and how to present the evidence at trial. The online predator follows the same grooming process as predators who do not use the Internet. First, the predator meets the child and builds trust through deception. Once the child develops trust in the perpetrator, the perpetrator often exposes the child to pornography to lower the child's inhibitions about sex. The Internet offers perpetrators the opportunity to groom multiple victims at the same time, because the technology allows perpetrators to communicate with potential victims without drawing public attention to themselves. The perpetrator may use photographic or other electronic equipment to capture and transmit images of the victim. Law enforcement officers must acquire probative evidence against the perpetrator, collecting and preserving all evidence of grooming, such as pornography, Web cameras, and other electronic equipment, so that prosecutors can present the evidence at trial to show the perpetrator's motivation.

The author describes the online grooming process, details evidence, and shows how to use the evidence in trial. Understanding the typical procedure that online predators follow when committing an offense enables prosecutors to use evidence of the process to build a solid case against online predators.

Harassment

Chaffin, Stacy M. "The New Playground Bullies of Cyberspace: Online Peer Sexual Harassment." *Howard Law Journal* 51, no. 3 (2008): 777–818.

Focusing on online sexual harassment among adolescent peers, the author of this study reviews legal cases that limit students' freedom of speech. Online peer sexual harassment occurs among teenagers when schoolmates, classmates, and friends use e-mail, cell phones, text messaging, instant messaging, personal Web sites, social-networking Web sites, and polling Web sites to make threats against and spread sexual rumors about their adolescent peers. The author argues that, although school administrators are already taking steps to prohibit offline sexual harassment, they also need to prevent online sexual harassment. In support of her call for action, Chaffin cites stories of children who have taken their own lives after experiencing online sexual harassment. Middle school and high school children form online groups, behaving in hurtful ways, such as dehumanizing a classmate, behavior that they are less likely to engage in outside of the group. Both groups and individuals often use social-networking Web sites, such as Facebook, My Space, and YouTube, to harass their peers.

Court decisions regarding students' rights to free speech—including *Tinker v. Des Moines Independent Community School District*,[1] which permits schools to discipline students for harmful speech; *Bethel School District No. 403 v. Fraser*,[2] which finds that students' expressive rights are not equal to those of adults; and *Hazelwood School District v. Kuhlmeier*,[3] which finds that schools need not tolerate students' speech if it impedes the school's basic educational mission—support the argument that online sexual harassment does not deserve protection under the First Amendment and that schools should regulate such behavior. Nevertheless, even though online sexual harassment is harmful to young people, most schools do not discipline students for engaging in it. The author believes that school administrators should treat online sexual harassment as a threat to adolescent safety and act to protect students from harassment.

---

[1] *Tinker v. Des Moines Independent Community School District*, 393 U.S. 503 (1969).
[2] *Bethel School District V. Fraser*, 478 U.S. 675, 678 (1986).
[3] *Hazelwood School District v. Kuhlmeier*, 484 U.S. 260 (1988).

The National Campaign to Prevent Teen and Unwanted Pregnancy and *CosmoGirl.com*. "Sex and Tech: Results from a Survey of Teen and Young Adults." Report, Washington, DC, 2008. http://www.thenationalcampaign.org/sextech/PDF/SexTech_Summary.pdf accessed March 26, 2009).

This study presents the results, including the questionnaire and responses, of a unique survey on text messaging of sexual content among adolescents and young adults. *Sexting* is adolescent slang referring to the sending or receiving of sexually suggestive images and text messages, often by cell phone. Participants in the study—653 teenagers, ages 13 to 19, and 627 young adults, ages 20 to 26—completed the online survey between September 25, 2008, and October 3, 2008. The researchers further analyzed some of the survey responses according to gender or age—for example, they segregated the responses of young adolescents ages 13 to 16. A considerable number of those 13 to 19 years old in this survey had sent, by electronic means, nude or seminude pictures or sexually suggestive text. Twenty percent of teenagers had sent nude or seminude pictures or videos of themselves, and 11 percent of girls ages 13 to 16 had sent such images. Thirty-nine percent of teenagers reported having sent sexually suggestive text messages, and 48 percent of teenagers reported having received such messages. Of those teenagers who had sent sexually suggestive content, 71 percent of the girls and 67 percent of the boys reported that they had sent the content to their boyfriends or girlfriends. However, 15 percent of those teenagers said that they had sent or posted nude or seminude pictures to people known to them only through online contact. Of those teenagers who had sent sexually suggestive content, 66 percent of the girls and 60 percent of the boys said that they had sent the material for fun or to flirt, and 12 percent of said that they had sent it because they felt pressured to send sexually suggestive messages or images. The study offers points for adolescents to consider before they send sexually suggestive content and suggestions to help parents speak with their children about sex and technology.

Lenhart, Amanda. "Cyberbullying and Online Teens." Research Memo, Pew/Internet and American Life Project, Pew Research Center, Washington, DC, June 27, 2007. http://www.pewinternet.org/~/media//Files/Reports/2007/PIP%20Cyberbullying%20Memo.pdf.pdf (accessed March 23, 2009).

In the national Parents and Teens 2006 Survey, researchers conducted telephone interviews, from October 23, 2006, to November 19, 2006, of 935 youth Internet users ages 12 to 17. Based on the reports of youth identified as victims of cyberbullying in that survey, the author reports the prevalence and pattern of online harassment and bullying among adolescents. The study found that 32 percent of the teenagers interviewed had been harassed online. Girls—especially older girls, ages 15 to 17—were more likely to have experienced online harassment than boys: 38 percent of the girls and 41 percent of the older girls had experienced online harassment, as compared to 26 percent of the boys. Sending or forwarding a private e-mail was the most common method of cyberbullying (comprising 15 percent of all cyberbullying incidents), followed by spreading rumors online (13 percent), sending threatening or aggressive messages (13 percent), and posting an embarrassing picture (6 percent). Older teenage girls, ages 15 to 17, were most likely to receive online threats. Teenagers who provided personal information on a social-networking site were more likely to be the target of harassment (comprising 39 percent of social network users) than those who did not use a social-networking site (23 percent). Fewer than one in three teenagers (29 percent of those interviewed) said that online bullying is more common than offline bullying, but 33 percent of the girls interviewed reported that online bullying is more common.

Ybarra, Michele L., and Kimberly J. Mitchell. "Prevalence and Frequency of Internet Harassment Instigation: Implications for Adolescent Health." *Journal of Adolescent Health* 41, no. 2 (2007): 189–95. http://www.unh.edu/ccrc/pdf/CV157.pdf (accessed March 20, 2009).

The authors describe the pervasiveness of mental health problems among youth who harass others on the Internet. The study is based on data from the Second Youth Safety Internet Survey, which the Crimes Against Children Research Center at the University of New Hampshire designed to study youth exposure to sexual content, solicitation, and harassment on the Internet. Between March 2005 and June 2005, researchers conducted telephone interviews of a nationally representative sample of 1,500 youth ages 10 to 17 years old. The authors of this article analyzed the survey results to identify the frequency with which the youth engaged in harassment activity, categorizing the offenders as 1) limited harassers who had engaged in harassment one or two times in the past year, 2) occasional harassers who had engaged in harassment three to five times in the past year, and 3) frequent harassers who had engaged in harassment six or more times in the past year.

The survey indicated that youth with behavioral and psychological problems were more likely than others to engage in online harassment. Frequent harassers were seven times more likely to have rule-breaking problems and nine times more likely to have aggression problems than those who did not harass others online. Boys were three times more likely to be frequent harassers than girls. Of those youth who harassed other youth online, 82 percent had been harassed online by someone else. Survey results also indicated that almost 30 percent of youth had harassed others online during the past year: 6 percent of youth had frequently harassed others via the Internet; 6 percent had occasionally harassed others online; and 17 percent had harassed others a limited number of times in the previous year. Because harassment events increase as psychological or behavioral problems increase, the frequency with which a youth engages in online harassment may be an indicator that mental health professionals can use to identify young people with psychological and behavioral problems.

Ybarra, Michele L., and Kimberly J. Mitchell. "Youth Engaging in Online Harassment: Associations with Caregiver-Child Relationships, Internet Use, and Personal Characteristics." *Journal of Adolescence* 27, no 3 (2004): 319–36. http://www.unh.edu/ccrc/pdf/jvq/CV63.pdf (accessed March 16, 2009).

This study examines psychosocial indicators present in preteen and teenage youth who use the Internet to harass their peers. The authors define Internet harassment as an intentional and overt act of aggression toward another person online, citing as examples, rude comments or intentional embarrassment. Researchers based this study on the First Youth Internet Safety Survey, conducted between September 1999 and February 2000. The Crimes Against Children Research Center at the University of New Hampshire designed the survey to study youth exposure to sexual content, solicitation, and harassment on the Internet. Researchers conducted telephone interviews with a nationally representative sample of 1,500 youth Internet users between the ages of 10 and 17.

Analyzing the results of the survey, the authors of this article attempted to determine whether online bullies differ from traditional, offline bullies. The study found differences and similarities between offline and online aggressors. Although boys commit most incidents of offline harassment, the number of boys and girls who use the Internet to harass their peers is almost equal. Both offline bullies and youth who harass others online often have multiple psychosocial issues: 51 percent of all bullies had been victims of traditional bullying, 44 percent had a poor relationship with their caregiver, 37 percent showed a pattern of delinquency, and 32 percent were frequent substance abusers. The authors suggest that mental-health practitioners, health-care providers, and educators need to address the mental health issues of those who use the Internet to harass others, as well as the mental health issues of those who are victims of online harassment.

Roban, Whitney. "The Net Effect: Girls and New Media." Executive Summary, Girl Scout Research Institute, Girl Scouts of the United States of America, New York, 2002. http://www.girlscouts.org/research/pdf/net_effect.pdf (accessed March 20, 2009).

This article, reporting a 2001 study of 1,246 girls, examines how parents can help their 13- to 18-year-old daughters use the Internet safely. Unlike other studies on the topic of adolescent Internet use, this study focused on teenage girls only and used a variety of methodologies, including small-group interviews, journals, written surveys, and an online survey. The study revealed that, although girls in this age-group know a lot about computers and the Internet, they still need and desire adult guidance. Fifty-eight percent of the girls reported that they themselves were the most computer-savvy person in their households. This finding indicates that, more than likely, not all girls are receiving pertinent Internet-safety information from their parents. Most girls said that they use their common sense to behave safely on the Internet. A majority of the girls—75 percent—said that their parents had set Internet rules for them, but 57 percent reported that they had broken those rules. The girls reported that parental rules included time limits on Internet use and prohibitions against online chatting, online shopping, and online romances or face-to-face meetings. Girls had also received prohibitive directives from their parents, such as "Don't give out personal information." However, the study suggests that girls need proactive advice as well. The girls reported their perception that their parents are concerned about the wrong things, such as the type of information the girls can access online, the kind of people they might contact, and their online behavior. The girls expressed their desire for their parents to teach them responsibility, to educate them about possible dangers, and to trust them to use the Internet safely.

The study concluded that parents should try to be more proactive in their relationship with their daughters. By attempting to understand their daughters' online lives and by developing trusting relationships with them, parents can learn to communicate better with their daughters and help them navigate positive and negative Internet experiences.

Cyberbullying

Kowalski, Robin M. "Cyber Bullying: Recognizing and Treating Victim and Aggressor." *Psychiatric Times* 25, no. 11 (October 1, 2008): 45–47.

In this brief article, the author describes the course of treatment that mental-health professionals offer cyberbullies and their victims. The author defines cyberbullying as bullying by means of electronic communications, such as instant messaging, e-mail, chat rooms, and cell phones, and defines eight specific forms of cyberbullying, such as harassment and exclusion. Therapeutic treatment begins with the psychological assessment of both victim and bully. First, the psychotherapist addresses the victim's immediate psychological needs, such as treatment for depression and anxiety. The psychotherapist reassures the victim that the bullying is not his or her fault. The psychotherapist follows up by teaching the victim strategies for protecting and asserting himself or herself in the future. However, the therapist provides a different therapeutic treatment to a cyberbully. Bullies need to accept responsibility for what they have done and understand the cost of their actions. Therapists work with cyberbullies to help them develop empathy for the pain they have inflicted, so that they understand the consequences of their behavior.

The author reports common warning signs of cyberbullying, such as anxiety, depression, poor health, poor school performance, and social isolation. In addition, the author suggests the need for further research, including case studies of interventions with cyberbullies. Given the frequency of teenagers' use of technologies to connect with one another, mental health professionals need to be aware of the dangers of cyberbullying.

Kowalski, Robin M., and Susan P. Limber. "Electronic Bullying Among Middle School Students." *Journal of Adolescent Health* 41, no. 6 (2007): S22–S30. http://www.wct-law.com/CM/Custom/Electronic%20Bullying%20Among%20Middle%20School%20Students.pdf (accessed March 24, 2009).

For this study, which focuses on electronic bullying among middle school students, 1,852 boys and 1,915 girls in sixth-, seventh-, and eighth-grade classes in the southeastern and northwestern United States completed 3,767 questionnaires. The authors chose these grades for the study because of the prevalence of traditional, offline bullying during these school years and the growing use of electronic media by middle school students. The study defined electronic bullying as bullying that takes place through Internet chat rooms, e-mail, instant messaging, text messaging, or Web sites. Eleven percent of the students reported being electronically bullied one or more times in the previous two months; 7 percent stated that they had bullied others electronically and had been the victims of electronic bullying; and 4 percent reported that they had bullied others electronically but had not been victims. Fifteen percent of the girls were the victims of electronic bullying, as compared with 7 percent of the boys, and sixth-grade girls were half as likely as seventh- and eighth-grade girls to be the victims of electronic bullying. The percentage of girl victims rose with each grade level, while the percentage of boy victims declined from seventh to eighth grade. The percentage of girl bullies who were also victims rose with each grade level, with the percentage of boy bullies who also were victims declining between seventh and eighth grade. Middle school youth most often experienced electronic bullying via instant messaging (66 percent), followed by chat rooms (25 percent), e-mail (24 percent), Web sites (23 percent), and text messaging (14 percent). The authors conclude that electronic bullying is a significant problem, suggesting that one potential means of preventing it is for schools to enact rules and policies prohibiting electronic bullying, in addition to those already in place to prevent offline bullying.

Moessner, Chris. "Cyberbullying." *Trends and Tudes*, April 2007, 1–4. http://www.harrisinteractive.com/news/newsletters/k12news/HI_TrendsTudes_2007_v06_i04.pdf (accessed March 23, 2009).

This study focuses on adolescents' reactions to cyberbullying. The National Crime Prevention Council commissioned this 2007 report by Harris Interactive, based on a national survey of 846 children ages 13 to 17. The council chose this age-group because parents tend to give children in this population less supervision than at other ages. The study defines cyberbullying as the use of the Internet, cell phones, or other technology to send or to post text or images intended to hurt or embarrass another person. The researchers asked young people about the prevalence of cyberbullying and their responses to it. More than four in 10 teenagers (43 percent) in this survey reported that they had experienced cyberbullying in the previous year, with the most common occurrence among those 15 and 16 years old. Although many middle school students (48 percent) and high school students (58 percent) reported that cyberbullying did not bother them, 58 percent of middle school students and 56 percent of high school students commonly responded to cyberbullying with anger. Girls (63 percent) reacted with anger more often than boys (48 percent). Seventy-one percent of teenagers surveyed believe that the most effective means of preventing cyberbullying is software that blocks site access, and 62 percent think that refusing to forward cyberbully messages is most effective.

Unique to this survey was a question about the school administration's role in preventing cyberbullying: only 33 percent of the teenagers felt schools should educate students about cyberbullying. However, 37 percent agreed that schools should have rules prohibiting cyberbullying. The study suggests that parents can help their children avoid cyberbullies by setting expectations for online behavior and monitoring their children's Internet activities.

Patchin, Justin W., and Sameer Hinduja. "Bullies Move Beyond the Schoolyard: A Preliminary Look at Cyberbullying." *Youth Violence and Juvenile Justice* 4, no. 2 (April 2006): 148–69.

In this preliminary look at the issue of cyberbullying, the authors describe the negative impact online bullying has on youth, providing the results of a survey conducted to determine the extent and nature of online bullying. The article defines cyberbullying as willful and repeated harm inflicted through the medium of electronic text. Cyberbullying causes public humiliation and embarrassment, which can lead to serious psychological, emotional, and social wounds. Adolescents' online interaction—their cyber life—often revolves around school. Events occurring at school are often the topic of cyber conversation, and cyber conversations often continue at school. The interaction between adolescents' school and cyber life has the potential to cause victims of cyberbullying greater public embarrassment than traditional, offline bullying.

To show the prevalence of cyberbullying among teenagers, the authors linked their Internet-based survey, conducted between May 1, 2004, and May 31, 2004, to a popular musician's Web site, and the vast majority of respondents were female. Therefore, the survey results may not apply to other populations. More than 47 percent of the 384 teenagers reported that they had observed online bullying, almost 30 percent reported having been bullied online, and 11 percent reported that they had bullied others online. The most common form of cyberbullying was to ignore someone online (accounting for 60 percent of cyberbullying incidents), followed by disrespecting someone (50 percent), calling someone names (30 percent), and threatening someone (21 percent). Telling the online bully to stop was the most common adolescent response (36 percent). The authors suggest that cyberbullying merits further academic inquiry to determine whether cyberbullies or their victims are at risk for future deviant behavior.

Strom, Paris S., and Robert D. Strom. "Cyberbullying by Adolescents: A Preliminary Assessment." *Educational Forum* 70, no. 1 (Fall 2005): 21–36.

This study, which examines cyberbullying in general, is unique in pointing out that cyberbullies threaten students and school staff and in describing steps that schools can take to repel this threat. The authors report an incident in which a student wrote about his hatred for a particular teacher on a Web site, commenting that neither students nor school staff feels safe when the community permits teenagers to cyberbully.

The authors suggest a number of ways for parents and school staff to minimize cyberbullying, including educational programs and improved communication with teenagers. The article reports that state departments of education are creating programs to educate teachers and school administrators about the problem of cyberbullying. The authors propose that, in addition, information technology staff in the school districts could design and deliver curriculum to educate students, teachers, and parents about appropriate cyber conduct and how to respond to online persecution. Schools could poll their students to determine whether they have experienced cyberbullying and what the extent of cyberbullying is in the school community. Adults, who generally use technology only as a tool, need to understand that adolescents consider technology, such as computers, text messaging, and chat rooms, an essential part of their social life. Parents need to develop close communication with their children, encouraging their teenagers to tell them if somebody bullies them online. Parents and adolescents need to report cases of cyberbullying to the police. Finally, the authors propose the need for new studies to determine methods of confronting and preventing cyberbullying.

www.ingramcontent.com/pod-product-compliance
Lightning Source LLC
Chambersburg PA
CBHW081809170526
45167CB00008B/3389